The Gate Theatre presents
THE SEXUAL NEUROSES OF OUR PARENTS
by **Lukas Bärfuss**

Cast (in alphabetical order)
Father **Brendan Hughes**
Fine Gentleman **Francis Lee**
Boss **Milton Lopes**
Mother **Éva Magyar**
Boss's Mother **Di Sherlock**
Doctor **Jack Tarlton**
Dora **Cath Whitefield**

Translator **Neil Blackadder**
Director **Carrie Cracknell**
Choreographer **Ben Duke**
Designer **Phil Brunner**
Lighting Designer **Katharine Williams**
Sound Designer **Gareth Fry**
Casting **Lucy Bevan**
Assistant Director **Leonie Kubigsteltig**
Production Manager **Peter Grant Williams**
Stage Manager **Victoria Eames**
Deputy Stage Manager **Katy Keggie**
Fight Director **Alison de Burgh**

For the Gate
Artistic Directors **Natalie Abrahami & Carrie Cracknell**
Producer **Evanna Meehan**
General Manager **Cath Longman**
Technical Manager **Nick Abbott**
Fundraising & Events Manager **Henriette Krarup**
Education & Access Manager **Lynne Gagliano**
Finance Assistant **Steve Woods**
GateInk Co-ordinator **Lloyd Wood**
Intern **Sheena Bucktowonsing**

The Gate is supported by

Principal Corporate Sponsor

The Company

Lukas Bärfuss (Writer)

Lukas was born in Thun, Switzerland in 1971 and now lives in Zurich. He is a playwright and novelist. His plays have been produced worldwide and most recently have included *Die Probe* (Münchner Kammerspiele, 2007), *Alices Reise in die Schweiz* (Theater Basel, 2005), *Der Bus* (Thalia Theater, Hamburg, 2005, Winner of Jury and Audience Award Mülheimer Theatertage), *Heinrich IV* (Schauspielhaus Bochum, 2002), *Vier Bilder der Liebe* (Schauspielhaus Bochum, 2002), *Othello* (Deutsches Schauspielhaus, Hamburg, 2001), *Meienbergs Tod* (Theater Basel, 2001), *Der Reise von Klaus und Edith durch den Schacht zum Mittelpunkt der Erde* (Schauspielhaus Bochum, 2001). *The Sexual Neuroses of Our Parents* was commissioned by Theater Basel and received its world premiere there in 2003. He is currently under commission at Thalia Theater, Hamburg and Dramaten in Stockholm.

Lucy Bevan (Casting)

Film includes: *The Golden Compass*; *St. Trinians*; *The Last Legion*; *Chromophobia*; and *The Libertine*. Theatre includes: *Camera Obscura* (dir. Jonathan Miller, Almeida); *The Boy Who Fell Into A Book* (dir. Tim Stark, English Touring Theatre).

Neil Blackadder (Translator)

Neil translates drama and prose from German and French. Last year his translations from German of plays by Maxim Biller and Rebekka Kricheldorf as well as Lukas Bärfuss were presented in staged readings in New York and Chicago. His work has appeared in journals including *Two Lines*, *Chelsea*, and *Absinthe*. He is also the author of *Performing Opposition: Modern Theater and the Scandalized Audience* and of numerous articles, and has served as dramaturg for new plays with Manbites Dog Theater in North Carolina and 24Seven Lab in New York. Neil grew up and went to university in England; since 1987 he has lived in the US, where he now teaches theatre at Knox College.

Phil Brunner (Designer)

Phil Brunner studied Design for Performance at Central Saint Martin's School of Art. After graduating in 2004 he worked as a stage manager and design assistant. In 2006 he was one of four winners of the Linbury Prize going on to realise his proposal for a production of *All Quiet on the Western Front* at Nottingham Playhouse.

Carrie Cracknell (Director)

Carrie is Artistic Director of the Gate Theatre. She trained at The University of Nottingham (History), The Royal Scottish Academy of Music and Drama (Directing) and The National Theatre Studio (Directing). In 2004 Carrie won The Bruce Millar Trust Award for directors. Directing credits include: *Rosie and Albie* development for The Young Vic Theatre. As Artistic Director of Hush Productions: *Stacy* (The Tron, Glasgow); *A Mobile Thriller* (BAC, National Tour, Bristol Old Vic, The Traverse, and The Harbourfront, Toronto) Winner Herald Angel Award; *Broken Road* (British Council Showcase, BAC) Winner Fringe First Award; *Death and The City* (The Tron); *The Hush* (BAC and The Ohio Theatre, New York) *Macbeth* (Djanogly Theatre, Nottingham). Hush is currently developing an adaptation of the film *Dolls* which will be co-produced with the National Theatre of Scotland in 2008.

Ben Duke (Choreographer)

Ben trained at Guildford School of Acting and London Contemporary Dance School. As a performer Ben has worked with the Darkin Ensemble, Maresa von Stockert's Tilted Co, Punchdrunk and Dog Kennel Hill. Ben is the co-founder of

Lost Dog who were awarded the Bonnie Bird new choreographers' award in 2005. Their work has been performed by Phoenix Dance Theatre and they have been commissioned to make work for From Here to Maturity, EDge and Transitions. Lost Dog's *The Drowner* was performed at the Place Theatre and the Edinburgh Fringe where it was nominated for a Total Theatre award. Their most recent work, *Hungry Ghosts*, was commissioned by the Place Theatre and was performed in April 2007.

Victoria Eames (Stage Manager)
Victoria trained at RADA. Theatre includes: *Bridgetower* (ETO – world premiere and upcoming national tour); *The Marriage of Figaro* (OTC, Dublin); *The Night of 1000 Voices 2005-7* (Royal Albert Hall & Odyssey Arena, Belfast); *Don Giovanni* (Amersham Festival); *The Playactor* (Old Red Lion); *Sweet Charity* (Theatre Royal, Drury Lane); *Crocodile Seeking Refuge* (National Tour); *An Evening With Michael Parkinson* (Theatre Royal, Windsor); *Fedora and The Queen of Spades* (Opera Holland Park); *Splendour* (The Cobden Club); *La Finta Giardiniera* and *A Night at the Chinese Opera* (Royal Academy of Music); *Still Waiting For Everything* (National Tour); *Aladdin* (Old Vic); *Into The Woods* (New Theatre, Oxford); *Krapp's Last Tape* and *The Zoo Story* (Bright Blue Productions); *Shopping & F***ing* and *The Kiss of the Spiderwoman* (Edinburgh Festival).

Gareth Fry (Sound Designer)
Gareth trained at the Central School of Speech & Drama in Theatre Design. His recent work as a sound designer includes: *Black Watch* (National Theatre of Scotland); *A Matter of Life and Death* (Kneehigh/ National Theatre); *How Much is Your Iron?*, *The Jewish Wife* (Young Vic Brecht Fest); *Noise of Time* (Complicite with the Emerson String Quartet); *Strange Poetry* (Complicite with the LA Philharmonic Orchestra); *Attempts on Her Life*, *Waves* (Olivier Award Sound Design 2007), *The Overwhelming*, *Theatre of Blood*, *Fix Up*, *Iphigenia at Aulis*, *The Three Sisters*, *Ivanov*, *The Oresteia* (National Theatre); *Harvest*, *Forty Winks*, *Under the Whaleback*, *Night Songs*, *Face to the Wall*, *Redundant*, *Mountain Language*, *Ashes to Ashes*, *The Country* (Royal Court); *Valencia* (Gate Theatre); *O Go My Man*, *Talking to Terrorists*, *Macbeth* (Out of Joint); *Astronaut* (Theatre O); *Romans in Britain*, *Shadowmouth* (Sheffield Crucible); *The Bull*, *The Flowerbed*, *Giselle* (Fabulous Beast Dance Theatre, Barbican Theatre); *Tangle*, *Zero Degrees and Drifting* (Unlimited Theatre); *Almost Blue* (Riverside Studios, Associate Director); *Living Costs* (DV8 at Tate Modern); *Phaedra's Love* (Bristol Old Vic/Barbican); *The Watery Part of the World* (BAC). More info at www.garethfry.co.uk.

Brendan Hughes (Father)
Brendan trained at New College of Speech & Drama and London School of Contemporary Dance. As an actor/ dancer he has worked with Moving Being in *The Influence of Moons on Tides* and *The Yeats Projects*, The English National Opera in *An Actor's Revenge*, and with London Contemporary Dance Theatre. He played Judas in Steven Berkoff's *Messiah* on European tour and at The Old Vic. Other theatre credits include seasons at Nottingham Playhouse, Liverpool Everyman, Theatre Clwyd, Westcliff, Plymouth and Stoke where he recently played Paul Sheldon in *Misery*. He wrote and performed his one man show *Myself Alone* at The Latchmere and Glaxa Studios in Los Angeles, where he also appeared in numerous independent films and television shows. Most recent TV includes *Hitler, The Rise of Evil* (CBS) and *Holby City* (BBC).

Katy Keggie (Deputy Stage Manager)
Katy trained at the Guildhall School of
Music & Drama. Theatre credits
include: *Angels in America* (UK Tour,
Headlong Theatre co-production with
Lyric Hammersmith and the Citizens'
Theatre); *The Chairs, Hair, The
Emperor Jones* (The Gate); *The
Woman in Black* (Fortune Theatre);
Communicate (Soapbox education
project at The Old Vic); *Games* and
After Liverpool; *Double Double* and
Bye Bye Blues; *The Linden Tree* (The
Orange Tree Theatre); *Starlight
Express* (UK Tour, Clearchannel).

Leonie Kubigsteltig
(Assistant Director)
Leonie trained at Universities of
Hildesheim/Bochum, Germany
(Drama/Comparative
Literature), Northern School of
Contemporary Dance, Leeds (BA
Contemporary Dance), and Central
School of Speech & Drama, London
(MA Movement Studies). Directing/
Devising credits include: *Petite Morte/
Grande Morte (Extracts from the
Insect Play)* (Shunt Vaults London);
You are Blood in My Mouth (Riley
Theatre Leeds); *Stealin' an Arm Ain't
No Crime (*Riley Theatre Leeds/
Yorkshire Dance Centre Leeds).
Collaborations/Movement Direction:
The Mother's Bones (Kath Burlinson
in association with the Weird Sisters,
M.E.N.'s award for 'Best Performance
in a Fringe Production', Escalator
East to Edinburgh); *The Speculator*
(Embassy Studio, Central School of
Speech & Drama). Assisting: *Long
Time Dead* (Paines Plough/Drum
Theatre Plymouth); *Studio Plymouth*
(Youth Music Theatre UK); *The
Beggar's Opera* (Trinity College
London/Blackheath Concert Halls).

Francis Lee (Fine Gentleman)
Francis trained at Rose Bruford
College of Speech and Drama.
Theatre work includes: *A Mobile
Thriller/Broken Road* (Hush
Productions – London, Edinburgh,
Toronto – Fringe First, Herald Angel
Awards); *The Cherry Orchard* (OSC -

Riverside Studios); *Flamingos* (Bush
Theatre); *Mother Courage and Her
Children* (Shared Experience – West
End and USA); *Fifty Revolutions*
(OSC – West End); *Boom Bang-A-
Bang* (Bush Theatre); *A Taste Of
Honey* (Bristol Old Vic); *A
Midsummer Night's Dream* (Northern
Broadsides); *Confetti* (Furious
Theatre – George Devine, TIME OUT
Awards); *The Taming of the Shrew*
(Ludlow Festival Theatre); *The Love
of An Angel* (Mermaid Theatre);
Fondant Fancies and Forbidden Fruit
(Old Red Lion Theatre). Film work
includes: *Me Without You* (BAFTA
nominated); *Topsy-Turvy* (BAFTA,
OSCAR recipient); *We Three
Warriors;* and *The Young Americans*.
Television work includes: *Clapham
Junction; Heartbeat; Emmerdale;
Midsomer Murders; Casualty; What
Else Is On?; Dinnerladies; Dalziel and
Pascoe; Eastenders; The Missing
Postman; The Governor; A Touch Of
Frost; Peak Practice; A Midsummer
Night's Dream;* and *Jackpot*.

Milton Lopes (Boss)
Milton started to act professionally in
1998 in Portugal. He worked with the
acclaimed Portuguese theatre
director Luis Miguel Cintra, in the play
Tieste, won Best Actor Award in
Angra do Heroismo International Film
Festival for his role as Domingos in
Fernando Lopes's film *The Dauphin*.
He started his international acting
career in the Edinburgh International
Theatre Festival, with the award-
winning Scottish writer and director
David Greig in the play *San Diego*,
and since then worked in different
countries and regions such as
Scotland, England (for Graeae
Theatre in Martin Sherman's *Bent*,
among others), France (in the film
Joseph), Mexico (David Mamet's
Duck Variations), Angola, and
Portugal.

Éva Magyar (Mother)
Éva trained at Budapest University of
Theatre and Film Art. Theatre credits
in England include: *Tristan and Yseult*

(Kneehigh Theatre at The National Theatre); *The Bacchae* (Kneehigh Theatre); *House of Deer* (The Shamans at BAC); *Ramayana* (Lyric Hammersmith). Choreography includes: *Tristan and Yseult*; *The Bacchae*; *Pericles* (Globe); *The Party* (BAC). Film includes: *The Understudy* (dir. Scott Crocker, USA). Éva is also a choreographer and director, and has a physical theatre company called The Shamans. They have won numerous awards including Herald Angel in Edinburgh, Best Director in Cairo, Critics Award in Poland, and The Independent Award in USA. In Hungary and abroad she has played in, choreographed and directed over 100 productions.

Di Sherlock (Boss's Mother)

Di is a founder member of the David Glass Ensemble and played Gertrude in the original cast version of *Gormenghast*. Other work includes: La Cubana's *Nuts Coconuts* (Barcelona, Edinburgh International Festival); *Dining with Alice* (Salisbury); *Cinderella*, *Blood Wedding* (Lyric Hammersmith); *Watch My Lips* (Charnock Company); *Kes* (York Theatre Royal); *Greek* (Westcliff); *Crimes of Passion* (Nottingham Playhouse); *The Rose Tattoo* (Peter Hall Company); *The Threepenny Opera* (Oldham Coliseum); *Vincent River* (BAC). She was a regular, Oona, on *Crossroads* (Carlton TV). Other credits include *Holby City*; *Doctors*; *The Vice*; *Beyond Fear*; *Secrets and Lies*; and *Hamlet the Movie*. She wrote and performed *Elizabeth the Virgin Queen* (City of London Festival) and *Who Killed Ramona Rhapsody?* a "musical murder mystery" for BBC Philharmonic/Radio 3. Di is associate director of The Generating Company (site-specific circus and aerial).

Jack Tarlton (Doctor)

Jack trained at LAMDA. Theatre includes: *Twelfth Night* and *The Taming of the Shrew* (Propeller – The Old Vic, Brooklyn Academy of Music,

The Watermill and world tour); *She Stoops to Conquer* (Manchester Royal Exchange); *Coram Boy* and *Once in a Lifetime* (National Theatre); *The Man Who* (Orange Tree); *Beasts and Beauties* (Bristol Old Vic); *Gagarin Way* (Primecut); *Romeo and Juliet* (Chichester Festival Theatre); *Howie the Rookie* (Fourth Road); *Afore Night Come* (Young Vic); *An Inspector Calls* (Garrick – West End); *A Month in the Country* and *Troilus and Cressida* (Royal Shakespeare Company). Television includes: *The Golden Hour* (Talkback Thames); *Dead Ringers, Doctor Who, The Genius of Mozart, Swivel on the Tip, Hearts and Bones, Wings of Angels, Life Support* (BBC Television); *Inspector Pitt Mysteries – The Cater Street Hangman* (Yorkshire TV/A&E). Film includes: *The Unscarred* (Time Film).

Cath Whitefield (Dora)

Cath studied at the University of Hull and Lecoq. Theatre includes: *The Caucasian Chalk Circle* (National Theatre); *Home East Lothian, Mancub, Gobbo* (National Theatre of Scotland); *Lost Ones* (Vanishing Point); *Charlotte's Web* (Citizen's Theatre); *Fierce* (Grid Iron); *A State of Grace* (King's Head).

Katharine Williams (Lighting Designer)

Katharine works primarily in the UK, with some international projects. Her designs have been seen in Hong Kong, New Zealand, Canada, the USA, Mexico, Ireland, Spain, Germany, Spain, Armenia and the Czech Republic. She has collaborated with artists and companies including Theatre O, Hush Productions, Hoipolloi, Chris Goode, Shams Theatre, Blue Hug, Stamping Ground Theatre, Inspector Sands Theatre, Tobacco Factory Bristol, Northern Stage and the Stephen Joseph Theatre. Katharine has worked with director Carrie Cracknell on *Dolls* and *Stacy* (Hush Productions and The National Theatre of Scotland) and *The Rage of Achilles*

(NSDF Ensemble); and collaborated with sound designer Gareth Fry on Theatre O's *Astronaut*. She is delighted to be returning to The Gate for the first time since 2002's *Death and the Ploughman*.

Peter Grant Williams
(Production Manager)
Having worked as a stagehand at New Theatre, Cardiff, for 10 years Peter toured with various shows both nationally and internationally for companies including Vanessa Ford Productions, Watershed, Middle Ground, Backrow, Live Nation in a variety of positions including Technical Stage Manager to Company Stage Manager. Shows have included *The Hobbit*; *Gumboots*; *Tapdogs*; *Bad Girls*; *Midnight;* and *The Railway Children*. Working as a Production Manager, he has sent shows on No.1 Tours throughout UK and numerous shows into the West End as well as smaller shows including BADA, Bath Theatre Royal, WNO and Opera Babes. Peter also regularly works for the RSC London Season as Head of Stage and has recently been Tour Manager for the Derren Brown show *Something Wicked This Way Comes* and worked on the Channel 4 programme of the same.

The Gate Theatre would like to thank the following for their help with this production: James Boult, Izzy Camball, Denis Charrière at the Swiss Embassy, Wotjek Duczmal, DVF (Latvian Welfare Fund), Ben Ellis, Undine Engelmann, Alicia Farrow, Emma Hardcastle, Julia Hicks, Johnston Pullen Ltd, Bill Knight, Gabby Leon, Raphael Martin, Jerry Otter, Daniel Rollings, Matthew Sedmak, Victoria Smalley, Graham Whybrow.

The Gate Theatre
The Gate, London's international theatre, is renowned for its inventive use of space and the exceptional artists it attracts. An environment in which artists can create first-class and original theatre, the Gate is a springboard for opportunity, allowing emerging artists to excel and make their mark. With an audience capacity of between fifty and seventy people, the space has challenged and inspired directors and designers for over 28 years, making it famous for being one of the most flexible and transformable spaces in London.

The Gate relies on artistic dedication and the generous support of individuals to produce the very best in international theatre. Never deterred by financial limitations, the Gate continues to break boundaries and challenge form. However, to do this we need your help. No gift is too small. For more information on the Gate's work and how to support it, please visit www.gatetheatre.co.uk.

The Gate Theatre would like to thank the following for their continued generous support: Eric Abraham & Sigrid Rausing, Rupert Christiansen, Kay Ellen Consolver & John Storkerson, Alexandra Emmerson, The Eranda Foundation, Edward Field, Nick Ferguson, Jenny Hall, Patsy Hickman, Jenni & Bill Hicks, David Kaskel & Chris Teano, Brian & Janet King, Jeremy Levison & Norma Miller, Tony Mackintosh, The Mercers' Company, Oberon Books, Kerri Ratcliffe & Doug Henderson, Royal Borough of Kensington & Chelsea, Jon & NoraLee Sedmak, Jake & Sandi Ulrich, Adriana & William Winters, The Worshipful Company of Grocers.

The Gate Theatre
11 Pembridge Road
London W11 3HQ
Box Office 020 7229 0706
www.gatetheatre.co.uk

THE SEXUAL NEUROSES OF OUR PARENTS

(*Die Sexuellen Neurosen unserer Eltern*)

Lukas Bärfuss

translated by Neil Blackadder

Characters

DORA
DORA'S MOTHER
DORA'S FATHER
DORA'S BOSS
DORA'S DOCTOR
A WOMAN, *the boss's mother*
The FINE GENTLEMAN

Settings

A fruit and vegetable stall
A middle-class flat
A doctor's office
A hotel room
A railway station
A campsite

Thanks are due to Barbara Frey and Judith Gerstenberg, director and dramaturg of the first production of this play.

This translation was sponsored by Goethe-Institut

1. Doctor's office. One pale afternoon.

Mother. Doctor. Dora.

MOTHER. During the day Dora would be listless, and then
sometimes in the middle of the night she'd squeal in a high-
pitched voice like a piglet. Once she had shut herself in and
locked the door. It was unbearable. And when the firemen
came and climbed in through the balcony with a ladder, all
at once she stopped, and said I ought to make coffee for the
men. And that it was cold outside and it was still night-time.

DOCTOR. I did hear that story.

The neighbours are lenient because of her sense of humour.

MOTHER. We tried everything, all the drugs, all the
combinations, we didn't give up until we'd found the right
thing. And so she became quieter and quieter: with my love
and the doctor's determination and stamina.

DOCTOR. It's nice that Dora's doing better.

MOTHER. I don't know if she's doing better. Sure, she doesn't
scream any more, but she also hardly ever laughs, she never
cries, she'll eat whatever's put in front of her. For two years
she hasn't really had a proper conversation, she just repeats
phrases, things she's picked up. Now and then she'll hum a
song, and no one knows where she got it from. Don't
misunderstand me. It's not that I'm ungrateful. But
sometimes I wish I could have the fits of rage back. Dora's
laugh, it was louder than my husband's laugh, and deeper.
You would think there was a sailor or a butcher inside my
little girl.

DOCTOR. Did you talk about this with my predecessor.

MOTHER. I didn't dare. He put himself to no end of trouble
with her. Dora was his passion, he tried everything. Wrote
about her. Came to the house if necessary, even on Sundays
and at night. He said he'd never come across a girl like her.
Who seemed at first glance like any other child. Just a hair's
breadth away from our world, and yet irretrievably cut off

from it. That man loved my daughter. She belonged to him more than to me. Now the good man is dead. I would like my daughter back.

DOCTOR. I don't understand.

MOTHER. I'd like you to take her off her medication.

DOCTOR. Have you thought this through carefully.

MOTHER. If something goes wrong, we'll still have this combination. It does keep her calm. We can always go back to that.

DOCTOR. Your daughter is dependent on the medication.

MOTHER. The last time I had my daughter was when she was a child. Now she's almost an adult. I've watched her body changing. I'd like to see how much her inside has changed. What's lying behind that face that always looks exactly the same.

DOCTOR. When I look over her medical history.

MOTHER. You don't need to read that to me. I know it well. I know it extremely well. I would like to risk taking some action. I have time. My husband works a lot, and I have no commitments to anything other than Dora. I'd like to try this with you. Or with another doctor.

DOCTOR. Can Dora understand me.

MOTHER. Of course.

DOCTOR. Hello Dora.

DORA. Hello.

DOCTOR. How are you feeling.

DORA *shows the doctor her tongue.*

MOTHER. That'll do, Dora.

Put your tongue in.

He's not going to examine you.

DOCTOR. What do you think of your mother's idea.

DORA. Dunno.

DOCTOR. She'd like to take you off your medication.

DORA. Ah.

DOCTOR. Do you not like that idea.

DORA. Dunno.

DOCTOR. Does it frighten you.

DORA. Dunno.

DOCTOR. You've got used to it.

DORA. Dunno.

DOCTOR. Do you understand what that is, medication.

DORA. Dunno.

MOTHER. Of course you know, Dora.

DORA. Oh yeah, sure I know.

DOCTOR. So.

DORA. We should ask Dad first.

MOTHER. I've discussed it with him.

DOCTOR. And what does he think.

DORA. Yeah, what does he think.

MOTHER. He's agreed to it.

DORA. Well then, what are we waiting for.

2. At a fruit and vegetable stall in the railway station. Trains can be heard in the distance. It's nearing evening.

Boss. Dora. Woman.

BOSS. I saw, Dora. I could see really well. I watched you all morning. Did you notice.

DORA. No.

BOSS. I don't take my eyes off you. Not for one second. I don't miss a single movement. How are you feeling.

DORA. Good.

BOSS. You're not focusing. Listen, Dora. Even if a new life is beginning for you now, there is an order to the world. So now you're going to put the cabbage back in the very last row. Look, it's a simple calculation:

How much does cabbage cost.

DORA. One ninety a kilo.

BOSS. Correct. And a family can live off a kilo of cabbage for two days. Two days. That could send us to the poor house, we'd have to close the business. Our rent's too high to be selling cabbage. But you would sell mangel-wurzels and fodder maize if I ordered them. We're not selling vegetables for making soup, Dora. That's not the kind of business this is! So: in the front row we have asparagus, watercress, salsify, but only if it's been washed, OK, mesclun lettuce goes in the front row, and renette apples from October into November, but from November on they count as storable fruit. And this shop doesn't carry fruit for storing. Sugar snaps do go in the front row, and snow peas, you're following, right, but not beans, at best beans go in the third row, and next to them turnips and those absurd Jerusalem artichokes. Those things will never make it into the front row at my place, even though in price they could match the watercress three times over. Only, the way the world works, even valuable things don't make it into the front row if they've got a face like a seed-potato that's been on the rack for three years. But you know all that, don't you.

DORA. Yes.

BOSS. So.

DORA. Dunno.

BOSS. Is it the medication.

DORA. Dunno.

BOSS. Why didn't she discuss it with me. It does affect me. I have an opinion about it. I work with you. She should have asked me what I thought. I resent your mother for this. This arrogant experimentation. You were fine, what does she need to change. I really resent her for it. Not you, Dora, you know that. I don't resent you for it. I don't resent you for anything. But when you're not focusing, when you're restless, I sense it. That's just how it is. It's as if I wasn't focusing myself. And if you're not taking any medication, to a certain extent I'm also not taking that medication. That's why it affects me if you're not doing well.

And we mustn't not be doing well.

The stall's already not doing well.

Silence.

We're going bust, Dora, haha, I can tell you.

DORA. Ah.

BOSS. And Mother will kick the bucket if we go bust. No question. She won't survive that. But fortunately she doesn't know.

WOMAN. What don't I know.

BOSS. Nothing, Mum, you don't not know anything.

WOMAN. Who is it you're talking with all this time.

BOSS. With Dora, Mum, I'm talking with Dora.

WOMAN. Leave the kid in peace for five minutes.

BOSS. There's something I have to explain to her.

WOMAN. Leave the girl alone.

Don't we have customers.

BOSS. Of course we have customers, Mum, of course we do. (*To* DORA.) She'd be in the ground within the week, no doubt about it, probably after just three days. Then she wouldn't be able to bother us any more. But then.

What then, Dora. What would become of you then. What would become of us. There'd be no more stall. And without the stall we can't see each other. But we can't get together. You know why.

You know, Dora, the two of us, it won't ever work, we're too different, it can't work, not in this lifetime, not in this world.

And that's why we need the stall. That's why you've got to focus, with or without medication.

We can't go bust.

Better for us to go to pot than to go bust.

Okay, back to work.

It's nearly closing-time.

So give me a kiss.

3. At home. By the bed. A night-light glows peacefully, and outside the window darkness lurks.

Mother. Dora.

MOTHER (*reading from a book*). There once lived a rich gentleman who owned the most beautiful suitcase in the whole land. In this suitcase there lived a frog. The frog was as big as a child, and he brought the gentleman luck. No matter what he took on, whatever work or task or love affair, the gentleman succeeded in everything, because he owned this magnificent frog. The frog also made the gentleman popular with everyone. The president of the land was his best friend and often invited him for dinner and discussed his problems with him. Later they drank schnapps and told jokes. And afterwards the gentleman went home to his frog who was just sitting there quietly in his suitcase. The frog made very few demands, every now and then he drank a little glass of apple wine, and he was quite satisfied if every day he got half-a-dozen ordinary dried bluebottles to eat. The gentleman got the flies from a shop that sold angling supplies, and the frog never wanted anything different. There was just one special thing that the frog desired. Once a week the gentleman had to bath him, and it had to be in a warm soapy bath. It could be ordinary soap, the most simple kind from the supermarket, two eighty for five. The man had to crumble a whole soap with a cheese grater, and then the flakes went into a shallow basin, and he added lukewarm water. He put the frog in, and the frog didn't do anything at all, didn't swim around in the soapy water and didn't splash about, just contentedly croaked a few times. After a quarter of an hour, the man picked up his lucky frog, held him under the running jet of water and rinsed away the foam from his green body. The frog let his light-green legs dangle, as if he was already dead, but the gentleman knew that his lucky frog liked this best of all. He dabbed him dry with kitchen paper. Then the frog, who was a lucky frog and made everything turn out well for the man, went back into the suitcase. (*To* DORA.) Are you sleeping.

DORA. I can't.

MOTHER. Why not.

DORA. The fairytale's too boring.

MOTHER. Don't you like frogs.

DORA. I don't like fairytales.

I never did.

MOTHER. And I go to the trouble of running around all the libraries so I can read you a new one every night. Why did you never say anything.

DORA. I couldn't.

MOTHER. Why not.

DORA. Dunno. I didn't care. I thought the fairytales were stupid, but I didn't care.

MOTHER. Does that happen to you with other things too. That you find them stupid and don't say anything.

DORA. Dunno. Yes. I don't really like trousers.

MOTHER. Which trousers don't you like.

DORA. All of them. I don't like any trousers.

MOTHER. But I only ever buy you trousers.

DORA. I prefer dresses.

MOTHER (*laughing*). Well then we'll simply throw your blasted trousers away.

DORA. All of them.

MOTHER. Yes, all of them.

DORA. I'd like to keep my jeans.

MOTHER. Then we'll throw all of your trousers away except the jeans. And tomorrow we'll go shopping for dresses.

DORA. Okay.

MOTHER. Oh sweetheart, I'm so happy. These doctors with their medications. It's time we finished with all that. No more pills, never again. I promise. Welcome, Dora, welcome to the world.

4. At the stall. One bright morning. It rained during the night.

Fine Gentleman. Boss. Woman. Dora.

FINE GENTLEMAN (*talking to* DORA *in a friendly manner*). On a day like today, the best thing of all for breakfast would be gooseberries. An irresistible fruit. For me. I can't explain it.

BOSS (*joining their conversation*). It's not the season for gooseberries.

FINE GENTLEMAN. You don't carry imported produce.

BOSS. Almost exclusively. Just no gooseberries.

No one eats them any more. Why don't you try an exotic fruit.

A pomegranate, for instance. Ripe and hand-picked.

FINE GENTLEMAN (*with a glance at* DORA). You like exotics, it seems, and not only when it comes to fruit.

BOSS. Ha ha ha, it's no big deal, I just like doing it, and Dora is a treasure. A real treasure!

FINE GENTLEMAN. One can see the girl's a treasure just by looking at her.

BOSS. Dora belongs to the business. She's sort of like my hobby-horse, if you know what I mean. It's amazing what you can learn from her. Hard to imagine. Incredible. Wonderful. It's not for nothing that our good Lord made all kinds of people.

FINE GENTLEMAN. Excuse me asking, but how much does the state support come to.

BOSS. State support.

What a joker.

Mum.

Come here a minute, would you.

WOMAN (*entering*). What is it.

BOSS (*laughing*). You won't believe it. The gentleman asks me to my face how much the state support comes to. To my face.

WOMAN. What state support.

BOSS. The state support for Dora.

WOMAN. Who would think about that. That has nothing to do with it. (*She exits.*)

BOSS. Either one feels the social responsibility or one doesn't. If it didn't cost anything, everyone would be a philanthropist.

It's the silent boycott that disturbs us.

No one says it directly to my face, but I'm not blind. They think that just because Dora is the way she is, she's not clean. They think my fruit and vegetables are not hygienic, not perfectly fresh.

Dora, come here a minute.

DORA *comes over to them.*

Show the gentleman your nails, would you.

DORA *shows the gentleman her nails.*

And.

FINE GENTLEMAN. Immaculate.

BOSS. Lift up your arms. If you don't mind.

DORA *does so.* FINE GENTLEMAN *inspects her armpits.*

Have a closer look. Do you see rings. You don't, do you. We make absolutely sure that our Dora is clean. But it's no use. People just think the girl is dirty and a breeding-ground for bacteria. I put the reports up from the health department, but it makes no difference. People don't want their produce to have been touched by a girl like Dora.

FINE GENTLEMAN. And yet these people are normal.

BOSS (*suddenly suspicious*). Which people.

FINE GENTLEMAN. I mean, people like Dora.

BOSS. Does that bother you.

FINE GENTLEMAN. Not at all.

BOSS. Don't you like Dora.

FINE GENTLEMAN. She has a nice smile.

BOSS. The medication's ruining her teeth.

Thank you, Dora, you can put your arms back down.

DORA *again does as she's told.*

Dora is a unique case. The researchers are interested in her, they know what she's worth in places that matter, and now they're taking her off her medication. The doctor hasn't noticed anything yet. But I have. You feel it. When you're as close as I am. Well I'll take it as it comes. However it turns out. Dora's my girl.

She opened my eyes to the beauty of the world. She showed me what's essential in life.

FINE GENTLEMAN. Would you mind giving me an example.

BOSS. That would be going too far.

FINE GENTLEMAN. Please.

BOSS. You'd have to experience it for yourself.

FINE GENTLEMAN. I'd give a lot for that.

BOSS. There are more people like Dora than we generally think. You just need to open your eyes.

So can I get you a pound of pomegranates.

FINE GENTLEMAN. Just the one will be fine.

BOSS *passes him the pomegranate and the* FINE GENTLEMAN *leaves.*

BOSS. I think you should watch out for that fine gentleman, Dora. For him and his gooseberries.

5. At the doctor's office. Early afternoon, and the world is full-up and sluggish.

Mother. Doctor. Dora.

MOTHER. It's like receiving a present. I've got my daughter back. She talks about herself, about what she likes and what she doesn't. She tells me about things from her day, what's bothering her, funny things. She shows her feelings. She's laughing again. For years we never laughed as much as we do now in one evening.

DOCTOR. Dora's not exactly lively.

MOTHER. It was the right decision. She's a human being again. When I look back over the last few years, I start to feel guilty, and I get angry with myself. And with that doctor and his damn ambition.

DOCTOR. He was convinced it was the right thing for your daughter.

MOTHER. Maybe Dora's been like this for a long time, healthy and happy, able to enjoy life. Behind that pharmaceutical curtain, all along there was this lively person.

DORA (*laughing*).
Behind that pharmaceutical curtain,
All along there was this lively person.

MOTHER. Yes, sweetie, what I said rhymed, by accident. How nice that you noticed.

DORA (*loudly*).
Behind that pharmaceutical curtain,
All along there was this lively person.

MOTHER. You see, now isn't that amazing.

DORA (*almost shouting now*).
Behind that pharmaceutical curtain,
All along there was this lively person.

MOTHER. That's good Dora, that's enough now, thank you.

DORA. Sure.

DOCTOR. How have the past few days been for you, Dora.

DORA. Me.

DOCTOR. Yes, tell me about it.

DORA. Really good. Honest. It's been a lovely time. I've enjoyed it. The right decision. Totally. Absolutely. I'm behind it one hundred per cent. And I've made progress, personally, I mean.

DOCTOR. Good, that's great.

DORA. And when I look back over the last few years, I start to feel – (*She suddenly stops talking.*)

MOTHER. You didn't finish the sentence. Finish the sentence.

DORA. Really.

MOTHER. Yes. You said when I look back over the last few years, I start to feel –

DORA. When I look back over the last few years, I start to feel guilty. And then I get really angry with myself. And with that doctor and his damn ambition.

MOTHER (*sadly*). Oh sweetheart!

6. In a hotel room. You can hear the pipes singing.

Fine Gentleman. Dora.

FINE GENTLEMAN. Come on in, please, have a seat. There, on the bed perhaps. I know, yes, it's rather cramped, please, don't hold that against me. And it hasn't been tidied up either. The maid doesn't do the room until the afternoon. If you really want it to be neat, you have to do it yourself. And I do like it to be tidy. But then I've also paid the maid, I mean, with the room, you understand, so I'm losing out if I tidy the room myself, you see, it's a dilemma. So, well. Would you like something to drink. Madam. A glass of wine, a beer, or champagne even. It's nice that you were able to decide so spontaneously.

DORA *doesn't reply.*

You're not exactly what they call a chatterbox, are you. Never mind, that doesn't bother me. I'm just wondering what a woman like you is doing at a fruit and vegetable stall. You don't need to say. If you'll permit me, I'd like to think this through. Where you could be from. Where your roots are. There's something Russian about you, isn't there, something of one of those last daughters of the Tsar, impoverished, dishonoured, stranded between potatoes and soup vegetables. That's where that nobility comes from, that tenderness, that suggestion of thin, aristocratic blood. Your family kept to itself for a long time, I'm sure of it, for generations they didn't mix with others, because the others weren't good enough, and that leads to this wonderful refinement of the features, this equilibrium, this quality of almost not being involved, royal, imperial. Am I totally on the wrong track here. They do say I understand something about human beings. And what is it shining in those sad eyes if not the memory of bloody Sundays and crowds of people shot to pieces. I can see the wide open spaces of the parks, stocks of trees hundreds of years old that have been chopped down in this icy winter, so the wood can be fed to the iron stove, the only thing left of the furnishings in the vast halls of the giant palace. Even the precious books have already been burned, as have the pictures and the ball-gowns. Now there's nothing left, just an old bear-skin that began losing its hair long ago. Wait, you don't need to say it, I see it in your eyes, how your family gathered around the fire, yes, and the faithful, old, pale, dried-up, sick servant pushes the very last log into the oven, and once it's burnt out, the cold of the universe breaks into the room and the soldiers storm in with bayonets attached, and in their looks there glimmers world history, and as we know that sets everything on fire, so that it blazes in the winter night, through which you flee, alone. Oh, my dear!

He takes DORA *in his arms, hugs her, looks her over, pushes her away again.*

How old are you.

DORA. Dunno.

FINE GENTLEMAN. Are you sixteen, at least.

DORA. Dunno.

FINE GENTLEMAN. Have you got some identification.

DORA. No.

FINE GENTLEMAN. And what's that you've got round your neck.

DORA. There's a note inside with my name on it, and our telephone number. And there's a ten-franc note. 'Cause one time I got lost and I'd forgotten my name.

FINE GENTLEMAN. But you're not a dog.

DORA. No.

FINE GENTLEMAN. No, you're an attractive girl. Stand up a minute, I want to look at you. That's good. Turn around. Nice. But you've got no arse.

7. At home. In the middle of the night, a candle burns and drips.

Mother. Dora. Father.

MOTHER (*crying, and rocking and comforting* DORA). My darling, you've got bruises all over you, you poor thing.

DORA. It's not so bad.

MOTHER. You don't understand what he did to you.

He even took the money off you, that horrible man.

DORA. He said he'd lost his wallet.

FATHER. Don't go believing everything people say.

DORA. Okay, Dad.

FATHER. Why did you go with him.

DORA. Because I'd never been in a hotel room.

8. At the doctor's. Early in the morning, you don't want to keep the day waiting.

Doctor. Mother. Dora.

DOCTOR. She came through it well. A few haematomas in the stomach area, grazes here and there, nothing that won't heal in a couple of weeks.

MOTHER. Bastard.

DOCTOR. I'm sorry.

MOTHER. Not you, the one who did this to her, he's the bastard.

DORA. You can't say that, Mum. He was nice to me.

MOTHER. Dora, he was only nice to you so that you'd go with him. What that man wants from you, it's nothing good. He took the best thing from you.

DORA. He'll give me the ten francs back, definitely, he promised.

MOTHER. Listen to me, Dora. You mustn't go there ever again, understand, never again, promise me.

DORA. And what'll we do about the ten francs.

MOTHER. The money doesn't matter. What matters is your health.

DORA. So am I not healthy.

MOTHER. Didn't you hear what the doctor said.

DOCTOR. You should believe what your mother says, Dora. She's right. There are some people who will take advantage of other people if they're too trusting.

DORA. Okay.

DOCTOR. There's still the question of whether to press charges.

MOTHER. I'd like to leave that up to Dora.

DOCTOR. Dora. Would you like to tell the police about it.

DORA. Will they get our money back.

MOTHER. Why do you keep going on about the blessed money.

DOCTOR. You would tell the police how the man hurt you.

DORA. It didn't hurt.

9. At the doctor's office. The mothers are already preparing the vegetables, the hungry fathers are putting up with their work, the children sit at school.

Doctor. Dora.

DOCTOR. It didn't hurt. Good, Dora, be glad, because that's not how it is for all girls the first time. That's nice. I don't begrudge you that. Neither do your parents begrudge you it, I'm sure, even if just now they're a bit upset, because you got a bit roughed up. But that's all right. You've had no practice, and when that's the case anyone would be okay with getting a few bruises. So everything's fine, Dora. Fundamentally. You don't need to worry. There's nothing bad about it, really there isn't, don't let anyone tell you different. That's how we come into being, all of us, imagine that, all in the same way, with and through this amazing thing. And that's why it feels good, as you found out for yourself. Even you should be allowed to experience it, yes, though they used to forbid it for people like you. For a long time they didn't want to believe that you have sexuality. But today we see it in a new way, differently. It's not only there for that, not only for having babies, definitely not, though some people still take that position. But you're not a Catholic, are you.

DORA *shakes her head.*

And your family isn't active in the Protestant church either, so we don't need to worry about that. Anyone and everyone should be allowed to do it, of course, everyone, so you too, Dora. Now you already know how it works, so I don't need to explain anything to you, I don't think, but if you have any questions, then please, come to me. Yes. Sometimes it's hard to go to your mother with these things, with certain questions, when it gets too personal, too intimate. So. What am I getting at. As with all things, with love there are a few rules you have to observe. Especially today, in these liberal times, you can't do without rules. That's the same for everyone, even I need rules that I can hold on to. Otherwise you can lose yourself in the great wide world, I see it every day, what happens to people who don't have an internal compass, whether it's because they have problems with authority or because they believe it would restrict their freedom too much. Restrict them. It's just the opposite. Without rules, without a compass, a person is restricted because the poor creature doesn't know what they should orient themselves by, where, yes, where they should turn. For it's not a question of things being forbidden, of course not, Dora, remember that, one must never allow the idea of the forbidden to enter one's head when it comes to amorous matters. Incidentally, the word amorous comes from the French and means having to do with love. So: don't ever think in terms of what's forbidden! Never think 'one mustn't do that,' 'that's not right,' and so on, and deny yourself something because of that. If you get into a situation, any situation, and you don't know should I or should I not, and a voice inside you shouts 'One mustn't do that, don't do it,' then watch out! Take care! Listen to that alarm! That 'one', it's the most wrong thing of all in love! You must protect yourself from that 'one' above all else! And do you know why? Because they're outside voices, the ones that argue 'one must not,' the voices of morality, yes, and if there is to be any morality at all in love, then let it only be your own, Dora.

Only one morality: Dora's morality.

Only one voice speaks the truth: Dora's voice.

Stand by the window, Dora, come, come over here by me, look
down into the street, go on, look at the faces of the people.
See, you can tell by looking at each one of them whose voice
he follows, whether it's his own or a voice from outside. That
man there with the dog and coat: an outside voice. That
woman there with the child and the umbrella: an outside voice.
Those tourists with the camera and the guidebook: onetwo-
threefourfivesixseveneightnineteneleventwelveandthirteen
outside voices, if we keep quiet we can hear them all the way
up here. (*Pause. Whispering.*) That murmuring, that wheezing,
do you hear that, and do you hear that grinning. (*Pause.*)
Look: her there with the pigtails and the short skirt: possibly
her own voice, could be, maybe, maybe. Yes, Dora, for every
ten followers you get at best one free person. I've never
maintained that it's easy, on the contrary, it's the most difficult
thing there is. But one must try to do it. You must try to do it,
Dora, you. What are they like, human beings. Do they want to
ignore the truth about themselves, can they live if they follow
the outside voices, the murmuring, the wheezing, the grinning,
doesn't it bother them if they're denying their true selves,
denying who they need and what they long for, do these
people lovingly close their eyes to themselves and to their
inner truth. Do people live like that, like cattle, Dora. No, they
want to find themselves, they want to recognise themselves,
they want to get close to themselves, that's what they're
looking for. And love, one's sexual life, for human beings it
serves a single purpose: self-recognition. A great, noble goal.
And it has nothing to do with what these days are referred to
as loose morals, walking around half-naked, getting the most
intimate body parts pierced, jumping from one bed into
another. People should do what they want to, I'm not going to
forbid them anything if it feels right to them. But does it feel
right to them. I don't think so, no. They have no compass, they
do believe they're doing what they want to, but they don't
know what that is. They have no idea what they want. Yes,
they think that what they want is the same as what they need.
Wrong, Dora, wrong and wrong and wrong again! If you only

go after what you seem to want, then you're just following the
loudest voice, and the loudest voice isn't necessarily your own.
In sum: don't trust the loud voice, it could be the one from
outside. (*Pause*.) Good. That's enough about all that. Let's talk
in concrete terms. In practical terms. Let's turn our attention to
civil and criminal law. You should know this much, Dora:
Never in front of other people. So it's best not to do it outside,
although that's not expressly forbidden, but only outside if it's
supposed to be something really special. So not too often. And
then it's also not a bad thing if someone should be watching
one time. The odd time. Really. So. And I wouldn't go to
places that are known as spots where people do it outside. If
it's known for it, that attracts people, strange people, and then
there's stuff lying around, you know. Like the campsite down
by the lake, it would be best not to go there. Just by going
there, you're already indicating an intention. And never on the
street, never on the street. Even though you might hear
something different, maybe, you know, about the entrances to
buildings, or behind rubbish skips or on traffic islands, what do
I know what's in these cheap romances. Do you read at all,
Dora.

DORA. I know how to read, but I can't remember any of it.

DOCTOR. Good, but I wouldn't do it there, it'd be better if you
didn't do that. Someone could always come by. That doesn't
have to be such a bad thing, definitely not, but when there's a
street there, the police react sensitively. And that really
wouldn't be good because certain things just happen to be
illegal, like causing a public nuisance and so on, you can end
up in prison or at least have to pay a fine. So not in stations,
not in the train, not in public squares, not in museums or
stadiums, not in the theatre, not in public toilets, and not on
other people's private property, that is, don't climb over some
fence and well, you know. That would bother you too, if
someone did it in your garden – in general, if you judge things
according to your own standards, then you'll be doing fine.
(*Pause*.) Now, I suppose that wouldn't bother you, would it,
Dora, if some guy hopped over your fence with his friend and
up goes the skirt and in her arse two three times in her pale
moonlit arse, where you can see the veins so nice under the
skin and it sways so nicely, right, that wouldn't bother you

would it, my little Dora. Hahaha. (*Pause*.) Fine, but the thing is, it does bother other people. As far as selecting your partners goes that's up to you in principle. Choose whoever you like. Of course he needs to want to too, but that's obvious. You can even choose a woman, and the age is not at all important. No, hang on, of course not, you mustn't with children, Dora, never with children, that's just as important as the thing about the public places, probably even more important. In any case it's just as illegal. And I would stay away from married men. It just leads to trouble, although it's not illegal and some people actually find it appealing, not altogether without reason, I must admit, but you have to be at an advanced level in these matters for that, because an amorous involvement with a married woman brings with it certain demands, organisational and financial. So that's not something for you, for the time being. And also with groups there aren't any laws, in theory, so you're okay there. But here too it's the case that too much of it is unhealthy. So not more than, let's say, two at once, and don't change your partner more often than once a week, or better still once a month. So. Well we've got quite a lot straight. Can you remember it.

DORA. Yes.

DOCTOR. So. (*He hands her a pill*.) Take one of these now. And then one in the morning, every day, and after twenty-one days you take a break. Your mother will show you how it works.

10. At the station. In the evening, at the hour when people are already or still at home and the streets stand empty.

Dora. Fine Gentleman.

DORA. Hello.

FINE GENTLEMAN. Hello.

DORA. How are you.

FINE GENTLEMAN. Fine.

Do I know you.

DORA. You owe me ten francs.

FINE GENTLEMAN. I'm sorry, you must be confusing me with someone else.

DORA. No, you confused me. You said I was Russian, even though I'm not Russian at all, but you said I might well be Russian without knowing about it. And then you fucked me. For about half an hour. Over there, in that hotel.

FINE GENTLEMAN. You certainly have an active imagination.

DORA. And then you spoke very loud and said things to me. But I've forgotten what you said, and you turned red, and then you pulled my hair and also you hit me a bit on the head. And then you sent me away. That's not right.

FINE GENTLEMAN. You've got a screw loose, haven't you.

DORA. I've got a bruise. (*She lifts up her sweater.*)

FINE GENTLEMAN. Stop it, you stupid thing. Are you trying to make trouble.

DORA. Don't send me away again. Take me with you. I'd like a chance to fuck for longer than just half an hour.

11. In a hotel room. Later, when the children ought to have been home long ago.

Fine Gentleman. Dora.

FINE GENTLEMAN. Don't make that face. It's got nothing to do with you.

One has to be careful.

Not all girls are as open as you.

DORA. You know other girls.

FINE GENTLEMAN. A few.

DORA. Do you fuck them.

FINE GENTLEMAN. What do you think of me. I'm the most faithful man in the world. I have only you. You're my girlfriend.

DORA. My mother's upset because of the money.

FINE GENTLEMAN. What money.

DORA. That you owe me.

FINE GENTLEMAN. You think I care about ten francs. Ten francs. It never even crossed my mind.

DORA. You have to give me the money back.

FINE GENTLEMAN. Is that why you came.

Do you only care about the money.

I haven't got any cash on me.

Take something for yourself out of my sample case.

You'll get the money back next time.

DORA *takes a bottle of perfume from the sample case.*

You seem to be an expert.

That's the most valuable one in the whole range.

DORA (*quoting*). The way the world works, even valuable things don't make it into the front row if they've got a face like a seed-potato that's been on the rack for three years. (*She smells the perfume.*)

FINE GENTLEMAN. Smells good, doesn't it.

DORA *nods.*

Do you like that.

DORA *nods and dabs some perfume on her neck.*

Do you know what you just put on your neck.

DORA. Nope.

FINE GENTLEMAN. Ox shit.

DORA. Hahaha, that's not true, it can't be.

FINE GENTLEMAN. Of course it is, they make the perfume from the shit of Siberian oxes.

It suits our fine Russian lady, this ox-crap scent, as if it was made for her.

And look at this soap.

What do you say to that.

What's our expert's opinion of this soap.

DORA. Pretty paper.

FINE GENTLEMAN. Yes. Well spotted.

And how does it smell.

Well. What does it smell of.

DORA. Of roses.

FINE GENTLEMAN. Of roses. Good.

The scent of roses for our fine lady, a rose soap for the Russian lady. With compliments.

And do you also know why the soap smells of roses.

DORA. So that the Russian lady smells of roses.

FINE GENTLEMAN. So that you can't smell the dead pigs the soap's made from. You fine ladies don't want to know it, but those little bath soaps packed up so nicely, they're made from pig fat. You kill off the pigs, cut the fat from the flesh, put it in a tub, cook it until it's clear and thin, then you add some caustic soda and finally some rose water, you wrap it in fine tissue paper and tie a ribbon around it so that it looks pretty and no one sees that there's nothing in there but a piece of dead pig.

DORA. Poor pig.

FINE GENTLEMAN. You like pigs, don't you. Well I can console you. It works with cows too.

DORA. And with frogs.

FINE GENTLEMAN. Theoretically. If there's fat there, you can make a decent soap from it. But even the best soap doesn't prevent women from smelling. I have a fine nose, Dora, believe me. I can smell ladies even through ox shit.

DORA. I don't smell.

FINE GENTLEMAN. No, you don't smell, you stink. You stink terribly.

DORA (*lifting her arms*). And we pay very close attention to make sure that our Dora is clean.

FINE GENTLEMAN. But I can smell it. I smelled it straight away when I saw you for the first time.

DORA. It would be a shame if you didn't touch the produce any more.

FINE GENTLEMAN. And what will the lady do so that the fine gentleman continues to sample her produce.

DORA. Dunno.

FINE GENTLEMAN. Don't wash. I don't like it when a woman smells of pig fat. If you wash yourself, I won't fuck you. That much I owe to my nose. And now come here to me, I want to make myself dirty on you.

12. At home. Over breakfast, with the smell of coffee and the hope that a new day brings.

Father. Mother. Dora.

FATHER. Do you have to let Dora use your perfume. God knows, I find it bad enough that you wear the same clothes and that you take her with you to your hairdresser. I'd like to be able to tell my daughter from my wife. Otherwise one of these days I'll accidentally commit an offence.

MOTHER. She just happens to like the same fashions as me. And also it makes it easier with the laundry. I've got enough on my plate with the housekeeping. (*Pause.*) Besides, I've never put perfume on Dora.

FATHER. Then our daughter is getting at your perfume without you knowing it.

MOTHER. Dora would never do that.

FATHER. She smells like the madam in a brothel.

MOTHER. My perfume doesn't smell like a brothel.

FATHER. Then tell me what your daughter smells like.

MOTHER (*goes to* DORA *and smells her*). You're right. That does smell like a brothel.

FATHER. Like I said.

MOTHER (*continuing to sniff*). That's not my perfume.

Too musty, it must have turned rancid.

I would never wear anything like that.

FATHER. Well if she didn't get it from you, who did she get it from.

13. At the fruit and vegetable stall. In a serious moment, without customers.

Woman. Boss. Dora.

WOMAN. It's perfectly normal for a young girl to wear perfume. I put perfume on when I was only fifteen. I don't see what's wrong with it. Just because Dora is the way she is, that's why she's not allowed to do it. She has to smell like an idiot. Her mother is a modern woman. So she claims, anyway. Why's she being so stubborn all of a sudden.

BOSS. She just wants to know who Dora got the perfume from. She's worried about her, that's all.

WOMAN. Who knows who she got it from. There are plenty of young men who know what you give a young woman as a gift.

BOSS. Dora is not a young woman.

WOMAN (*to* DORA). Don't listen to him, they wanted to stop me from doing it too when I was young. Father beat me half to death. I didn't care. Better a black eye than to go around with no perfume on, that's what I used to say. Don't get confused, dear, our Lord in heaven wants us to adorn ourselves. By making yourself look nice, you're praising him and his works.

BOSS. Mum, please, come on, did she get it from you or not. If she got it from someone else, I'm the one who'll get into trouble. Because I didn't keep an eye on her. And I promised I would keep an eye on her. You know what happened. With that bloke. And then she'll take Dora away from me. And who'll sell my stuff then. You certainly won't.

WOMAN. It can't do her any harm to get the chance to see something else, something other than always just your fruit and veg.

BOSS. What's wrong with my fruit and veg.

WOMAN. After all, it is a classy perfume. The customers like it. You can tell her that. The young lady is just showing that she has the good taste her mother lacks.

BOSS. As far as I'm concerned the kid can stink. Who cares about the customers. I don't want any eager beavers here. Did

I hire a beauty queen. Dora's supposed to sell vegetables. I look after everything else.

14. At home. Mother's out.

Father. Dora.

FATHER. Sweetheart. Look at what a state you're in.

DORA. A bit messy.

FATHER. You haven't washed for a week.

DORA. No.

FATHER. You used to like having a bath so much. Really hot and with lots of foam, remember.

DORA. Sure.

FATHER. That was always the high point of your week.

DORA. We shouldn't look back, Dad.

FATHER. People will stop liking you.

DORA. The main thing is that you love me.

You do love me, right.

FATHER. You're my daughter.

DORA. Do you like me.

FATHER. Why are you asking that.

DORA. You've never told me if you like me.

FATHER. You're an attractive girl.

DORA. And you're an attractive guy.

15. In a hotel room. Time forgets, the moment lingers, people grow tired.

Fine Gentleman. Dora.

FINE GENTLEMAN. What are you gawping at.

Don't gawp like that.

Or at least say something.

You can make a fellow nervous, being so quiet afterwards, when before you go at it like the devil. If I don't watch myself with you, there'll be nothing left of me.

DORA. Did I do something wrong.

FINE GENTLEMAN. Not at all, on the contrary. That's the thing. I'm just wondering who showed you.

DORA. You.

FINE GENTLEMAN. Me.

DORA. I just do what you do.

FINE GENTLEMAN. You do it willingly.

DORA. I willingly do what you do.

FINE GENTLEMAN. All right, that's enough talking. Off you go.

DORA. No.

FINE GENTLEMAN. Out, I'm telling you.

I've still got things to do.

DORA. I'm staying.

FINE GENTLEMAN. Are you deaf.

Your parents must be worrying about you by now.

DORA. I don't have to be home until it gets dark. It's still light.

FINE GENTLEMAN. What did you tell them so they'd let you go off on a Sunday.

DORA. That I was visiting my boyfriend.

FINE GENTLEMAN. And instead you snuck out to see me. You little liar.

DORA. I didn't lie.

FINE GENTLEMAN. So you think I'm your boyfriend.

DORA. Don't you want to be. You only have to say.

FINE GENTLEMAN. How many boyfriends have you had before.

DORA. None.

FINE GENTLEMAN. So I'm your first man, right.

DORA *nods*.

You'll have me crying in a minute.

DORA. Why.

FINE GENTLEMAN. You're lying to me.

DORA. I'm not lying.

FINE GENTLEMAN. You really never had anyone else before. Is that true. Oh Dora. You're giving me that. You dear thing. To me. And I'm so awful to you, my little angel. I do nothing but the filthiest things and I'm so mean to you.

DORA. You're not mean to me.

FINE GENTLEMAN. I am, Dora, I am, I'm mean to you. I haven't deserved you at all. Not something as delicate as you.

No one's ever given me that before.

DORA. Was it the first time for you too.

FINE GENTLEMAN. It was the first time for me with someone for whom it was the first time. Before this, Dora, I'd only ever had, you know, old, used-up women, and whores.

DORA. What are whores.

FINE GENTLEMAN. Women you pay for it.

DORA. Do you also pay them.

FINE GENTLEMAN. Far too much, Dora, far too much.

DORA. Pay me too.

FINE GENTLEMAN. For what.

DORA. For the fucking.

FINE GENTLEMAN. You don't understand, Dora. Come here a minute. You aren't a whore. No, my dear, you're something special. You're an angel. Heaven sent you. From now on I'm going to be good to you. I promise. I'll show you what I haven't ever shown anyone. What I'm really like. There, can you feel that, that's me, and you're doing that with me. My angel. I won't send you away. There's no way I'll ever send you away again. Am I crazy. I'm not going to send an angel away.

16. At the doctor's office. It cooled down overnight.

Doctor. Mother.

DOCTOR. Dora's pregnant.

MOTHER. That's impossible.

DOCTOR. Yes.

MOTHER. Never.

DOCTOR. Very probably.

MOTHER. That miserable wretch.

DOCTOR. You know him.

MOTHER. I'll find him, I swear I will.

DOCTOR. And then.

MOTHER. I'll make sure that the bastard pays for the child.

DOCTOR. If he's in a position to do so.

MOTHER. Why would he not be in a position to do so.

DOCTOR. He would have to have work.

MOTHER. You're always assuming the worst case scenario.

DOCTOR. Mmm.

MOTHER. So are we supposed to pay for the child.

DOCTOR. Well.

MOTHER. If I have to bring it up, I at least want to get paid for doing so. (*Pause.*) When I start to think about it.

A baby again as well as Dora.

Back to square one.

What will people think.

It'll be like in a zoo.

DOCTOR. Like in a zoo.

MOTHER. I meant like in a place where they breed them, with Dora's child there.

DOCTOR. We can't know what the child will be like.

MOTHER. What do you mean.

DOCTOR. Whether it will be healthy.

MOTHER. Why should it be healthy.

DOCTOR. There's a chance it might be.

MOTHER. Now you're going to the opposite extreme.

DOCTOR. We mustn't limit ourselves in choosing what measures we want to take. We do still have time.

17. At home. The night-light is turned on, but there's little comfort to be had.

Mother. Dora.

MOTHER. Listen to me, Dora. I won't be reading you any bedtime stories today, do you understand.

DORA. Okay.

MOTHER. Let's talk about some important things, shall we.

DORA. Sure.

MOTHER. Do you understand what's going on.

DORA. No.

MOTHER. What did the doctor tell you.

DORA. I'm pregnant.

MOTHER. Why didn't you take the pill.

DORA. These doctors with their medications. It's time we finished with all that. No more pills, never again.

MOTHER. It isn't a medicine, Dora. The pill is so that you don't have a child. I take them too, you know. (*Pause.*) And what do you think should happen now.

DORA. Dunno.

MOTHER. You don't know. I don't know either. But someone has to know.

Silence.

We could still get rid of the child.

DORA. Okay.

MOTHER. You would agree to that.

DORA. No big deal.

MOTHER. It is a big deal.

An abortion is a sad thing.

DORA. Then I don't want an abortion.

MOTHER. But maybe it's the only solution.

Or tell me who's going to look after the baby.

DORA. Me.

MOTHER. That's a lot of really hard work.

DORA. Because the kid's also got a screw loose.

MOTHER. Who's got a screw loose.

DORA. I've got a screw loose.

MOTHER. If you believe that, you can give up on yourself right now.

DORA. Okay.

MOTHER. Who did you get this 'okay' from anyway.

DORA. Dunno.

MOTHER. So please can you make a suggestion.

DORA. We could give it to someone who can't have children.

MOTHER. That's a nice idea, but I don't think it's a gift anyone would be very pleased with.

DORA. Then let's wait until it's born and then we'll kill it. Seriously.

MOTHER. That's forbidden, Dora.

DORA. We won't tell anyone. We'll tie it to a tree and then we won't have anything more to do with it.

MOTHER. You're awful.

DORA. No big deal.

MOTHER. We can't do that, Dora. Trust me.

DORA. Then I don't know.

MOTHER. Would you listen to Dad.

DORA. I always listen to Dad.

18. At home. On Sundays, Dad has time.

Father. Dora. Mother.

FATHER. That's women's business. What do I know about it.

It's indecent.

Why didn't you take care.

DORA. Dunno.

FATHER. Not you, for God's sake.

You let the child have too much freedom.

MOTHER. I don't need you to criticise me.

Try suggesting something.

FATHER. We don't need anyone to suggest anything.

Look, it's clear to all of us what we need to do.

And there's not much to it these days, or so I've heard.

MOTHER (*bitterly*). You haven't got a clue.

FATHER. No, I really haven't. But I do know what the only solution is. And so do you.

And so does Dora.

Don't you, Dora.

DORA. Of course I do, Dad.

19. At home. Outside it's a lovely day.

Mother. Dora.

MOTHER. Oh darling, was it very bad.

DORA. Not at all. There's not much to it these days.

MOTHER. You are brave.

DORA. When the doctor came in with the hose, I thought we were going to fuck. But then instead of pushing in, it sucked. That's not bad either. And it sounded like when you suck out the last bits in a glass with a straw.

MOTHER. You're disgusting.

DORA. Okay.

MOTHER. And now.

DORA. I'd like a coffee.

MOTHER. You're allowed that.

DORA. Yes. But I'm not allowed to fuck for ten days.

MOTHER. You should just about be able to manage that, don't you think.

DORA. No.

MOTHER. If I was in your position I'd stick to the doctors' advice.

DORA. Sure.

MOTHER. I'm serious about this, Dora. Otherwise you'll get a terrible infection.

DORA. Or I'll bleed to death.

MOTHER. That's what the doctors said.

DORA. That's what I figured.

'Cause there was so much blood.

20. At the doctor's office. In a light-hearted mood.

Doctor. Dora.

DOCTOR. You have a good constitution, Dora, I congratulate you.

DORA. Dunno.

DOCTOR. Your body is doing well. Tough as leather.

But I can't see how things look inside you.

DORA. Well there's a ball of cotton-wool, about this thick, a bit like a cock, only it isn't a cock, it's so that the blood doesn't run into your knickers, and that's why I have to be patient with my insides, but in ten days it'll be okay to get back into the fucking.

DOCTOR. That's not what I mean, Dora.

Don't you feel sad.

DORA. I always feel sad.

Except when I'm fucking.

DOCTOR. Do you sometimes think about the baby.

DORA. Gone is gone.

DOCTOR. You don't waste time thinking about trivial things, do you.

DORA. Right, doctor, that's right.

DOCTOR. I don't believe you, Dora.

DORA. Oh.

DOCTOR. Even you have feelings.

Let's play a game, shall we.

DORA. Sure.

DOCTOR. I say a word, and you say the first thing that goes through your head. Is that clear.

So I say: Fire.

DORA. Fire.

DOCTOR. You aren't allowed to say fire.

DORA. But that's the first thing that went through my head.

DOCTOR. You have to say a different word.

DORA. I see.

DOCTOR. So. Fire.

DORA. Fire.

DOCTOR. All right, let's stop there.

21. At the stall. It's a cool morning.

Woman. Dora.

WOMAN. How are you.

DORA. Fine.

WOMAN. Well then. I knew it. You won't mope around for long, will you.

DORA. Definitely not.

WOMAN. We're made from the same stuff. Just don't let them get you down. That's what they want, these men. I always bounce back too. Ha! That would be a laugh.

DORA. Hahaha!

WOMAN. Hahaha! (*Pause*.) Was it unpleasant.

DORA. Far from it.

WOMAN. You see.

The things you hear about it, real horror stories. And even if they were true. If it is unpleasant, that's exactly why you shouldn't mope about it. We're strong women. Shall I tell you a secret. I nearly got rid of him too. Then you wouldn't have a boss now.

DORA. Do you regret it.

WOMAN. You might think so. But why should I regret anything. I didn't want to marry his father. That's why I had to finish with him. Well. What are you going to do. Things keep going. Of course I'd rather have remained independent. But it was illegal, and going abroad, I couldn't afford that. Anyway. I just took things as they came, and didn't let it get me down.

DORA. Exactly. Bouncing back.

WOMAN. Life is all about ups and downs. What's the point in worrying about it all. You have to look ahead. Especially as a woman. Otherwise you go mad, stark raving mad. (*Pause*.) Dora, just between you and me, pay a bit of attention to your personal hygiene.

DORA. Don't you like this perfume.

WOMAN. Since you're asking so directly, no. I like the French perfume, but you can hardly smell it any more under yours.

22. In a hotel room. Before it's quite become a habit.

Dora. Fine Gentleman.

DORA (*quoting*). Well you've really gone and done something there, my dear Herr Gerber.

FINE GENTLEMAN. I'm sorry.

DORA. A proper mess. You should have seen it.

FINE GENTLEMAN. I can imagine.

DORA. Yes, and who's going to clean up after you.

FINE GENTLEMAN. I didn't do it on purpose.

DORA. If it had been up to me, I'd have kept the baby.

FINE GENTLEMAN (*laughing*). That would have been something, you and me and a child.

A pretty little family, imagine.

DORA *gets undressed*.

What are you doing. What do you want.

DORA. To fuck a new child. But this time we won't tell anyone. Otherwise it'll get sucked away again.

FINE GENTLEMAN. People will notice in any case.

DORA. I'll pull my stomach in. Look, like this.

She does so.

FINE GENTLEMAN. You won't keep that up for nine months.

23. At the fruit and vegetable stall. When no one's looking for once.

Dora. Woman.

DORA (*handing the woman a piece of paper*). I know how to read. But I can't remember any of it.

WOMAN (*reading*). 'Couple in their middle years, clean, fit, open to all things it's fun to do together, seeking a bachelor, clean and fit, to join them in escaping the everyday.'

You chose the wrong section, Dora. Look under 'Men seeking women' if you're looking for a relationship. (*Pause.*) Or do you maybe have a boyfriend.

DORA. Dunno.

WOMAN. I can tell by looking at you, you have a boyfriend.

And that's where you got the perfume from.

DORA *nods*.

Then he's generous. That was really good perfume.

DORA. Dunno.

WOMAN. He must be the adventurous type, if you already need to escape the everyday after two weeks. Either that or he's a swine.

DORA. And what does it say here.

WOMAN (*reading*). 'I read your ad with interest. I'm an experienced bachelor, clean, fit, healthy, slightly dominant, not bi, with my own caravan for getting together without being disturbed, no financial interests, but above average in size and staying power. I enclose a photo.' (*She looks at the photo.*) I have to hand it to you, you've thought of everything. But if I were you, I wouldn't go there.

This is a man for someone who's advanced, a beginner wouldn't have any fun with him. (*Pause.*) And if your boyfriend already wants to share you with someone like that after two weeks, then maybe he'll want to share you with everyone.

DORA. No big deal.

WOMAN. At some point he'll demand money for it, Dora, and then you'll end up on the streets. There are lots of bad people in the world.

DORA. Worse than me.

WOMAN (*laughing*). You're not bad, Dora. You're a lamb.

24. At the stall. A little later.

Boss. Dora.

BOSS. And who do we have here.

DORA. It's me, Dora.

BOSS. I see that. Just the same as ever. Only a bit pale still, around the nose. (*Pause.*) I could get angry with you, Dora. You know why.

DORA. I can imagine.

BOSS. Good.

Are you in pain.

DORA. Nope.

BOSS. That's good. But to begin with I won't have you emptying any crates.

DORA. Thanks, boss.

BOSS. What did I tell you. Watch out for him and his gooseberries, I said. And what does she do, straight away she runs off with this bloke. And who's going to be held responsible afterwards. (*Pause.*) You don't know who cares about you. Was I ever mean to you.

DORA. Nope.

BOSS. And why don't you do what I tell you.

DORA. I'm sorry, boss.

BOSS. You should thank your mother. If it weren't for her you'd be out on the street now.

DORA. My mother is sweet.

BOSS. I'll say. But I'll tell you one thing. I'm not running a rehab centre here. I have to make money. From now on you'll do exactly as I tell you.

DORA. Whatever you say, boss.

BOSS. From now on we're a team again. Give me a kiss.

DORA *does what he asks her to, and she does it a bit more intensively. She grabs the back of her boss's head and won't let go.* BOSS *pushes* DORA *away.*

(*Indignantly.*) Holy Mother of God.

DORA. You didn't do it very well.

BOSS. I didn't do it very well.

DORA. You need to use the whole of your tongue. Flick it around, and don't poke around in my gums with the tip.

BOSS *slaps her face.*

I don't know that technique. Have you got a hard-on.

25. At the station. After a lot has been shattered.

Fine Gentleman. Dora.

FINE GENTLEMAN. Hello Dora. Why so sad.

DORA. All I did was kiss him.

FINE GENTLEMAN. Who did you kiss.

DORA. My boss.

FINE GENTLEMAN. Usually one doesn't kiss one's boss.

DORA. Why not.

FINE GENTLEMAN. You just don't.

DORA. He always kissed me. And I never kissed back. Until today. And now he's given me the sack.

FINE GENTLEMAN. Don't worry yourself about it, Dora. Most people have been sacked at some point.

DORA. You too.

FINE GENTLEMAN. No, not me, not yet.

I did, however, go bankrupt once, and that's worse.

Do you have any plans yet. For this free day.

DORA. We can't. Have to wait ten days.

FINE GENTLEMAN. Dora. We could just take a walk for a change.

26. By a lake. Near a campsite where one goes if one has certain intentions.

Dora. Fine Gentleman.

DORA. There's Dad's car. Over there next to the bachelor's caravan.

FINE GENTLEMAN. What bachelor.

DORA. The middle-aged, clean, clean-shaven, well-hung bachelor.

FINE GENTLEMAN. Are you having a relationship, Dora.

DORA. I'm not, but my mum is.

FINE GENTLEMAN. There are people there. I just saw a woman.

DORA. That's my mum.

FINE GENTLEMAN. And what's she doing here.

DORA. She goes to the campsite because she has certain intentions.

FINE GENTLEMAN. Well look at that, the girl knows all about it.

27. At home. After they have hurried, only to perhaps get there in time after all.

Mother. Dora. Father.

MOTHER. You're home already.

Why aren't you at work.

DORA. I got the sack. No big deal. Everyone's been sacked at some point.

MOTHER. He gave you the sack. (*Pause.*) He can't do that without talking to me first. He'll be getting a phone call from me, and on Monday you're going back to work.

FATHER. Perhaps we should first hear exactly what happened.

DORA. All we did was kiss.

FATHER. Who did you kiss, Dora, who did you kiss.

DORA. The boss. But he didn't like it and he spat on the ground, and then he sacked me and then we went for a walk.

MOTHER. For a walk.

DORA. My boyfriend and me.

MOTHER. And held hands I suppose.

DORA. Nope, we didn't hold hands, but we did go to the campsite.

FATHER (*faintly*). Aha. To the campsite.

And what were you doing there.

DORA. Nothing special.

It's true, right, Dad, Mum is not a beginner.

FATHER. Well that depends in what area.

DORA. The boss's mother said a beginner wouldn't have any fun with someone like that, but Mum was having fun, I could see that really clearly.

FATHER *hits* DORA *in the face*.

Will you take me with you when I'm not a beginner any more.

FATHER *hits her again*.

No big deal. You were there too.

FATHER *hits her again*.

Okay.

No big deal.

28. At the doctor's office. The doctor's taken time out on a Sunday.

Doctor. Dora.

DOCTOR. That was crude of you, Dora. Crude and insensitive.

DORA (*eating dried apricots*). Sure.

DOCTOR. I understand your father.

Anyone's hand would have slipped.

DORA. Of course.

DOCTOR. You're making things very hard for your parents at the moment, Dora.

You're not washing, you got the sack.

Your mother doesn't know what to do with you any more. (*Pause.*) You've turned into an animal.

DORA. My mother is a good, dear woman.

DOCTOR. Why do you do these things.

DORA. Dunno.

DOCTOR. Well give it some thought, come on.

DORA. I didn't know that my parents fuck.

DOCTOR. Everyone does.

DORA. So why doesn't anyone know.

DOCTOR. They do know.

DORA. Why am I not allowed to.

DOCTOR. You are, Dora.

DORA. Okay.

DOCTOR. I just assumed.

DORA. You should have told me.

DOCTOR. I didn't consider it my job.

DORA. Why. Don't you fuck.

DOCTOR. I prefer to use another word for it, Dora. I call it making love.

DORA. What's the difference.

DOCTOR. It's not so rough.

DORA. I like it rough.

Otherwise I don't feel anything.

Don't you like it rough.

DOCTOR. Not necessarily.

DORA. Why not.

DOCTOR. It's not just about me. It's also about my wife.

DORA. And she doesn't like it rough.

DOCTOR. This is going a bit far for me, Dora.

My wife and I, we love each other. It's a give-and-take thing, understand. A back and forth, not just an in and out. Sexuality is a whole world, an ocean, you see. You sit together over a nice meal, you listen to music, light a candle, pay each other compliments.

DORA. What are compliments.

DOCTOR. When you say nice things to the other person, that they're attractive and that you like them. And perhaps, if both want to, in the end you become intimate.

DORA. Well then Mum wasn't making love, she was fucking. She didn't eat anything, and there were no candles.

DOCTOR. That's her business, Dora.

DORA. Okay.

DOCTOR. Don't those things make you feel sick.

DORA *shakes her head and offers the doctor an apricot. He takes one. As he does so she hums a song.*

DORA. I like you. You can explain the most difficult things.

DOCTOR. I'm glad, Dora.

DORA *takes off her sweater.*

Good, Dora, but that'll do.

DORA. Why not.

DOCTOR. Stand up. Get dressed.

DORA *does so. And falls back down.*

29. Doctor's office. Late is the hour, and tired.

Doctor. Mother.

DOCTOR. Dora told me about what she experienced at the campsite.

MOTHER. That's my private affair.

DOCTOR. It's on your daughter's mind.

MOTHER. My husband and I want to also have a private life. A life without her. There's no way we can keep something secret for ourselves. It's hard enough stopping Dora from picking up on everything. She's at home all the time. At least until recently. So we make our little excursions together. Are we supposed to deny ourselves something because of Dora.

DOCTOR. No one's asking that of you.

MOTHER. I'm wondering if she did that before too. In the past three years. Did she secretly watch everything and not let on.

DOCTOR. What could she have watched.

MOTHER. How do I know what she could have watched. Our life.

DOCTOR. Dora lives with you. She doesn't need to watch in order to know about your life.

MOTHER. I suppose you tell your children everything.

DOCTOR. I don't have any children.

MOTHER. Then I'll tell you what it's like. You don't show your kids your whole life. Certain things you keep to yourself.

Why am I even talking about this here, with you. It's got nothing to do with you, and there's nothing to be said about it.

DOCTOR. Well now she's found out about it.

MOTHER. She snooped around. What did she get for it.

DOCTOR. Your daughter is not doing well.

MOTHER. She's not had any medication for weeks.

30. At home. In the morning, at Dora's bed.

Mother. Dora.

MOTHER. If you whine, I'll leave.

DORA. Okay.

MOTHER. You see where your lack of restraint gets you.

DORA. Why didn't you tell me.

MOTHER. What didn't I tell you.

DORA. That you fuck.

MOTHER. Because it's none of your business.

DORA. In my whole life I've never seen anything so beautiful. You looked like a real angel.

MOTHER. Be quiet.

DORA. I want to wear clothes like that too, those shoes and stockings.

MOTHER. They wouldn't suit you.

DORA. I had this nice feeling as I was watching you, it was even nicer than fucking, and then us two idiots, we fucked too, right there, because we couldn't stand it, though I was supposed to have waited for ten days, but you were inside, where it was warm, and we were outside, but it was still nice, a bit cold, but fucking warms you up. And now I have to die.

MOTHER. Why don't you keep your stupid mouth shut just for a while.

DORA. But Dad was there too.

So it can't have been anything bad.

And your face was so happy.

MOTHER. You don't understand anything.

DORA. Explain it to me.

MOTHER. No.

DORA. Please.

MOTHER. Another time, maybe.

DORA. Don't you love me any more.

MOTHER. What gives you that idea. You just shouldn't stick your nose in things that are none of your business.

DORA *laughs*.

What's there to laugh about.

DORA. That's funny. Sticking your nose in things. (*Pause*.) And now I have to die.

She keeps quiet.

MOTHER. That's enough, stop with this performance.

DORA. I love you, Mum. Have a good life.

MOTHER. Stop it, Dora.

DORA. Sure.

MOTHER. Dora.

Silence.

Dora. Stop this nonsense.

Dora.

31. At home. Alone, in a lonely but quiet hour, waiting makes you feel forgiving.

Mother. Father.

MOTHER. Somehow I always thought about those wildlife films that show how an animal with even the slightest injury doesn't stand a chance. The lion steps on a thorn, he can't hunt any more, that's that. Deformed offspring get eaten by the mother there and then. Just one foot with six toes will do it. Because a living thing with six toes is not fit for life. We humans are different.

FATHER. I'm not accusing you of anything.

MOTHER. There's still time for that. (*Pause.*) I thought I was the one who was sick, not Dora.

I felt as if I'd been poisoned.

FATHER. I don't understand.

MOTHER. Didn't you ever go to church in the country. You often see these families with four or five children, like the pipes of an organ, and they're all wearing glasses with such thick lenses, mother, father, daughters, sons. And of course you wonder, why did those two of all people get together when they've both got something wrong with their eyesight. It's irresponsible, surely. (*Pause.*) Why did we get together.

FATHER. I always thought it was because we loved each other.

MOTHER. Oh, that's why.

No, because we don't look that way to each other. It didn't look to me as if you were ill.

FATHER. I'm as fit as a fiddle.

MOTHER. There must be something wrong with you, or else you wouldn't have a daughter like that.

FATHER. A variation from the norm doesn't mean an illness.

MOTHER. But darling, we're already variations from the norm. We just didn't know it. Our genes are bad, because of radiation, the hole in the ozone, pollution, because our parents were too closely related.

FATHER. But our parents aren't remotely related to each other.

MOTHER. You never know.

If we had known how bad our genes were, we wouldn't have got together.

FATHER. You don't need to take all the blame on yourself.

MOTHER. I'm not.

FATHER. You are. You always rule out everything else.

MOTHER. Just accept it, can't you.

FATHER. We had some lovely moments with her.

MOTHER. Name one second when you didn't wish we had a normal, healthy child.

FATHER. I wished it for Dora. For her to be healthy.

MOTHER. Oh stop talking rubbish, that's something you couldn't even imagine. A healthy Dora. Dora with a rosy complexion and a slim figure. Dora with normal bowel movements and not always constipated from those damn medications. Dora with even a single complicated train of thought. Dora not either shouting all over the place or else going for days without saying anything. A Dora who just once, just for one minute, is perfectly clean, no stain on her blouse, no streak in her underwear. You couldn't even imagine that. And if you try to, then there's nothing left of Dora. Be honest for once in your life.

FATHER. Healthy or sick, all human beings have their dignity.

MOTHER. Dignity. Whatever. If you had known when I was pregnant how the child was going to turn out, would you have still wanted to have Dora. Be honest.

FATHER. Well we didn't know then.

MOTHER. These days we would know it. (*Pause.*) At the beginning I consoled myself with the idea that you and I would outlive Dora. Just be patient, trust in nature, nature would work it out for us. And then we could have another try. But the child was tough, wasn't she, tough as leather. She clung onto her existence, and then suddenly we weren't young any more and the child was actually more alive than us. Screwed around, got pregnant.

Would you have thought Dora could get pregnant. I mean, just anatomically.

FATHER *can't reply, because* DORA *enters.*

DORA. Hello.

MOTHER. We thought they wouldn't let you out of the hospital until tomorrow.

DORA. Tough as leather.

32. At the doctor's. A new week begins, and you give yourself another chance.

Dora. Doctor. Mother.

DORA. Today I'd like to tell you something. My boyfriend says it's fine with him.

DOCTOR. Well.

DORA. We'd really like to have a baby, if that's possible, please.

MOTHER. I've told her again and again to put the idea out of her head.

DORA. He'd like to have a family.

He has work and earns good money.

It would be enough for three.

MOTHER. Why for three.

DORA. For father, mother and child.

MOTHER. You're going to move out.

DORA. I'll come and visit often. Every weekend, definitely, I promise.

MOTHER. That man doesn't really mean what he says.

DORA. He loves me.

MOTHER. What makes you think you know that.

DORA. You can feel these things.

DOCTOR. Well since it seems like this lover really is serious, we should give the gentleman a chance. Maybe he's not so bad after all.

MOTHER. Didn't you see what he did to her.

DORA. That's my private affair.

DOCTOR (*to* MOTHER). You've got to look at things head on: you can't change the original situation and think it won't have any consequences. Sometimes it's precisely the medications that you don't take that have the strongest effect.

MOTHER. We went way too far.

DOCTOR. Let's approach the problem quite openly. Dora. What do you think your boyfriend would say if you asked him to come here with you.

DORA. Dunno.

DOCTOR. Tell him we'd like to get to know him. So that we can discuss, the three of us, how it might work with the young family.

33. In the hotel. Time seems to be running out.

Fine Gentleman. Dora.

FINE GENTLEMAN. What exactly did they say.

DORA. We're going to discuss how it might work with the young family.

FINE GENTLEMAN. Great. And why do I need to be there.

DORA. You're the father.

FINE GENTLEMAN. Why does that mean I should go to a doctor. With you. And what'll your mother be doing there. It's our private affair, right.

No, no, there's something behind this, Dora. They're setting me up.

DORA. My mother doesn't want to fuck you. She said so herself.

FINE GENTLEMAN. They want to pin something on me. They don't like that you're my girlfriend. Do you understand, these days it doesn't take much to end up in prison. Don't you read the newspaper.

DORA (*annoyed*). I know how to read.

FINE GENTLEMAN. I know that, I know you can read. Very well, in fact.

DORA. The doctor's a sweet man. And you already know my mother.

FINE GENTLEMAN. How am I supposed to know your mother.

DORA. There was only one woman in the caravan. That was my mother.

FINE GENTLEMAN. That doesn't mean I know her.

DORA. But she knows you. You and your sort. She hates you.

FINE GENTLEMAN. That's what I'm saying. They're setting me up.

DORA. I have a plan.

Bring your case with you. That way they'll see that you have a job and that you don't have a screw loose. And at the end you can give Mother some perfume.

FINE GENTLEMAN. Not all women like my perfume.

DORA. Everyone's corrupt.

FINE GENTLEMAN. You don't have a very good opinion of your mother.

DORA. My mother is a sweet woman.

FINE GENTLEMAN. So. You've thought it through pretty well up to there. But how does the rest of your plan go.

DORA. Then we fuck a child, and then we leave it in until it comes out, and then we give it a name.

FINE GENTLEMAN. And I bet you know what name.

DORA. We give him the most beautiful name in the world.

FINE GENTLEMAN. I can't wait to hear this.

DORA. Our child will be called Dora. That's the most beautiful name in the world.

All you have to do is come with me to the doctor's. Will you come.

FINE GENTLEMAN. I'm thinking about it. I promise. I'll sleep on it. Come here.

DORA *does so. They kiss.*

You reek. You stink like an old goat. What kind of an angel are you. To think that there's something like you in this world. Come.

They kiss again.

34. At the doctor's. Time gets stretched and stretched into long threads until finally it rips.

Doctor. Dora. Mother. Father.

DOCTOR. We've waited long enough.

DORA. He'll be here soon.

MOTHER. You've been saying that for half an hour.

DORA. He'll come. Definitely.

MOTHER. That's it, I've run out of patience. Come to your senses, Dora. Your boyfriend is a piece of shit who shows no responsibility. You got mixed up with a sadist. That's what it looks like. He mistreats you for his own fantasies. So be it. It can happen. Your business. Except that you almost died, you were this close to being dead now.

DORA. He loves me.

MOTHER. You don't know what love means.

DORA. I feel it.

DOCTOR. This is no use. We need a solution that everyone can live with.

One at a time. Dora. What's most important to you.

DORA. I'd like to have a Dora.

DOCTOR. Isn't love the most important thing to you.

DORA. A Dora that everyone can love. Who gets fucked. Who everyone loves. Like me. I'm loved by everyone.

DOCTOR. Good. Well at least that's a clear wish. But I'll be honest with you. We don't know what your child will look like.

DORA. Like me.

DOCTOR. It will look similar to you, you're right there.

DORA. This Dora will be ugly, like me. But that's no big deal. Only it should have better teeth. Here in front there's one wobbling around again. See. That won't stay in much longer.

DOCTOR. Answer a question for me, Dora.

Do you think you're healthy.

DORA. I've got a bit of a cold coming on.

DOCTOR. You're not healthy, Dora.

DORA. So what do I have.

DOCTOR. Nothing serious. You're a good, strong girl. But your child could have a much, much worse illness.

DORA. And then it will die.

DOCTOR. Perhaps.

DORA. Ah.

DOCTOR. You don't want that.

DORA. No.

DOCTOR. You see.

DORA. I'd like to not have any medication, if that's possible, please.

DOCTOR. We understand that, Dora, and we respect it too. There are, thank God, other solutions. There's nothing to it any more, really. Lots of modern, clever women who don't want to have children have it done. They don't allow their femininity to be defined only through being a mother. And by the way, even men do it.

DORA. Does Dad do it too.

FATHER. I've thought about it.

DORA. If Dad does it, then I want to do it too. (*Pause*.) Will I have to wait for ten days after again.

DOCTOR. I'm afraid we won't be able to avoid that. But afterwards there'll be no more limits placed on you. You'll be able to lead your life just as you choose. As a complete woman.

MOTHER. And you can even reverse it, right.

DOCTOR. Absolutely, of course. If all the details fall into place. And if it should really be necessary, then one could look into it and see if that's a possibility.

35. In the hotel. In the twilight hour.

Fine Gentleman. Dora.

FINE GENTLEMAN. Don't make that face. It's got nothing to do with you. I was held up. I do have to make a living, you know.

DORA (*with a suitcase in her hand*). At first they were only going to cut through the tubes, but then the doctor said it's healthier if they clean out the uterus while they're at it. Since I don't need it anyway, and you can so easily get cancer there. And if I want children, they'll simply reverse it.

FINE GENTLEMAN. Is that what they told you, Dora.

DORA. Yes. Now I'm a complete woman. And modern.

FINE GENTLEMAN. They tricked you. An operation like that can't be reversed.

DORA. No.

FINE GENTLEMAN. Absolutely not.

DORA. So what about our children.

FINE GENTLEMAN. That's it for them now, I'm afraid.

DORA. Ah. (*She cries.*)

FINE GENTLEMAN. Don't cry, little Russian. Maybe it's better this way.

DORA. So don't you want a family any more.

FINE GENTLEMAN. It's not so important.

DORA *takes off her clothes*.

What are you doing. Stop it.

DORA. Aren't we going to fuck.

FINE GENTLEMAN. No, your insides will be all full of blood.

She snuggles up to him.

Get off, you stink.

DORA. It's not my fault. They washed me. In the hospital. While I was asleep.

If you don't want to fuck me, then would you mind beating me a little.

FINE GENTLEMAN. Why should I beat you.

DORA. Because it's fun.

FINE GENTLEMAN. Is that what you go around telling people. That I beat you.

DORA. That's what I told my mother.

FINE GENTLEMAN. You shouldn't tell lies to your own mother, Dora.

DORA. I don't tell her lies.

FINE GENTLEMAN. I have never yet beaten you, my little Russian. Not one single time. (*He hits her.*) Now I'm beating you, Dora. Do you see the difference.

DORA. No. Will you explain it to me.

FINE GENTLEMAN (*hitting DORA again*). Is it fun.

DORA. It's okay.

FINE GENTLEMAN (*hitting DORA again*). Well, and now, do you see the difference now.

DORA. It hurts a bit.

FINE GENTLEMAN. A bit, yes. (*He hits her again.*)

The difference is that I don't fuck you afterwards.

That's the difference.

DORA. Okay.

FINE GENTLEMAN. And now get your things together.

DORA. So aren't we going to Russia.

FINE GENTLEMAN. Of course we're going to Russia. I just have to take care of a few things first. You go on ahead, we'll see each other there.

DORA. But I don't know the way to Russia.

FINE GENTLEMAN. Go to the station. There must be a sign there somewhere. You can read.

DORA (*nodding*). Will you come soon.

FINE GENTLEMAN. Of course. I wouldn't keep you waiting now, would I.

Wait. (*He gives her a bill.*)

There's your ten francs back. So that we're even.

DORA. If only mother could see this. She said I'd never see that money again. And that we're going to Russia, she didn't believe that either and didn't want to let me go. And Dad said this moment had to come some day, but Mum cried, and then he said that if you let go then your hands are free, but Mum cried, and Dad said we prepared her well, and Mum packed my suitcase and cried and she didn't even stop when I promised I'd send her a postcard from Russia.

FINE GENTLEMAN. She'll be so pleased when she gets it.

Now off you go, otherwise you'll miss your train.

DORA. Will you kiss me.

FINE GENTLEMAN. No, Dora, if I kissed you it would be a farewell. I'll kiss you in Russia, my little princess, I'll kiss you in Russia.

Fin de la bobine.

A Nick Hern Book

The Sexual Neuroses of Our Parents first published in Great Britain in this translation in 2007 as a paperback original by Nick Hern Books Limited, 14 Larden Road, London W3 7ST, in association with the Gate Theatre, London, by arrangement with Wallstein Verlag, Germany

Die Sexuellen Neurosen unserer Eltern copyright © Lukas Bärfuss
Copyright in this translation © 2007 Neil Blackadder

Lukas Bärfuss and Neil Blackadder have asserted their right to be identified respectively as the author and translator of this work

Cover design: Ned Hoste, 2H

Typeset by Nick Hern Books, London
Printed and bound in Great Britain by Biddles, King's Lynn

A CIP catalogue record for this book is available from the British Library

ISBN 978 1 85459 579 9